MILLIONAIRE SECRETS

THE REAL BLUEPRINT TO SHORT TERM RENTAL SUCCESS

NOELLE RANDALL,
MPS, MBA

Copyright © 2021 by Noelle Randall

All rights reserved. In accordance with the U.S. Copyright Act of 1976, the scanning, uploading, and electronic sharing of any part of this book without the permission of the publisher constitute unlawful piracy and theft of the author's intellectual property. If you would like to use material from the book (other than for review purposes), prior written permission must be obtained by contacting the publisher at books@waltonpublishinghouse.com Reviewers may quote brief passages in reviews.

Walton Publishing House
Houston, Texas
www.waltonpublishinghouse.com
Printed in the United States of America

The advice found within may not be suitable for every individual. This work is purchased with the understanding that neither the author nor the publisher is held responsible for any results. Neither author nor publisher assumes responsibility for errors, omissions, or contrary interpretations of the subject matter herein. Any perceived disparagement of an individual or organization is a misinterpretation.

Brand and product names mentioned are trademarks that belong solely to their respective owners. Library of Congress Cataloging-in-Publication Data under

ISBN: 978-1-953993-18-2 (Paperback)

ISBN: 978-1-953993-19-9 (Digital/ Ebook)

NOELLE RANDALL
COACHING

Disclaimer: All documents in this book are intended for the use of the reader as a sample to edit only and not to copy. These documents remain the property of Noelle Randall Coaching and thus may be confidential and/or legally privileged or otherwise protected.

CONTENTS

Dedication 8

Chapter 1.
The Business of Short-Term Rentals 9

    Statistics on Airbnb 14
    How Airbnb Started 15
    How Does it Work? 15
    The Concept 16
    Airbnb Rental Arbitrage 17

Chapter 2.
Getting Started- The Beginning Steps 19

Chapter 3.
Finding the Perfect Property 25

    Properties to Rent 26
    Decide on the Location 28
    Create Your Property Criteria 28
    Search for Property Owners 29
    Revenue Sharing 33
    Closing the Deal 34
    Corporate Leases 35

Chapter 4.
Preparing Your Property 55

    Home Signage and Welcome Binder 58
    Remove Items from the Home 59

Chapter 5.
Listing Your Property 74

    Property Description 76
    Listing Your Property 77
    Quick reference list of websites 77
    Pricing Your Listing 78
    Booking Calendar 79
    Weekends vs. Weeknight Rates 79
    Seasonal Pricing and Holiday Sales 80

Chapter 6.
Managing and Growing Your Business 82

    Trusted Partners 84
    Growing with Guest Reviews... 85
    How to Get More Five Star Reviews 86
    Welcome Your Guest 87

Chapter 7.
Ready, Set, Go! 88

Acknowledgments 91

About the Author 92

Connect with Noelle... 94

*Don't listen to negative people,
you can make as much money as you want!*

Noelle Randall

Hello Future Millionaire,

Welcome to BNB Riches. My name is Noelle Randall, and I am a real estate entrepreneur, mentor, and mom of seven. I am passionate about helping everyday people just like you earn millions of dollars. I am so excited that I get to do what I love and help others tap into unlimited wealth and resources. As a real estate investor, I have seen first-hand the change in our economy. With this shift, there has been a surge of new millionaires in the short-term rental market. After witnessing the success my students and so many others were having, I couldn't let such a great opportunity pass without investing in the home-sharing economy. I jumped into short-term rentals, and now I have tons of short-term rental properties and have earned millions of dollars in the process. This new form of investing broadened my horizons to how to create additional streams of revenue with a daily influx of cash. Today I rent apartments, condominiums, houses, and even timeshares. Now it's time for me to share these secrets with you.

To Your Success,

Noelle

DEDICATION

I want to dedicate this book to my students because I am forever learning from them. I want to point out one student, in particular, Jeremy G. Jeremy is the student that taught me about renting apartments for Airbnb. He is the true catalyst to my BNB Riches!

CHAPTER ONE
THE BUSINESS OF SHORT-TERM RENTALS

Everything you need to know about the short-term rental business to help you start making your millions is in this book. I will give you the secrets and share the tips that most gurus won't tell you because they believe if they teach you too much, you will become their biggest competition. I am going to share how you can use the properties owned by others to make a substantial amount of wealth. If you have connected with me through my YouTube page, any of my social media platforms, or a live event, you have noticed that I have given you the resources and knowledge for what it ultimately takes for you to be successful in real estate and business, as I'm often known for oversharing free secrets on these platforms long before you ever join one of my programs. I do this because I really want you to win and learn how to create a wealth legacy for your family. I do this because I want you to obtain trusted information that really works in today's economy. I do this because I operate in the law of abundance and not scarcity, and I know there is more than enough wealth to go around. *Do you believe in this law of abundance?* I hope so. I want you to create the life of your dreams because you deserve it.

In this book, I will be teaching you how to make profits and cash flow six figures without owning any property. Yes, you read that correctly. I want to teach you the secrets to BNB riches that I use, as well as teach my students to help them earn additional streams of income by leveraging sites like Airbnb, VRBO (Vacation Rentals by Owner), and HomeAway. One of the biggest secrets that I have learned on my journey to making millions is how to make money with other people's money and properties. Many of my millionaire and even billionaire friends use this strategy to create unlimited wealth. If you have ever thought about starting in real estate but felt limited because you don't have the capital or the resources, I am deflating any limiting beliefs that you may have in this area. You don't need to use your own money to create unlimited wealth. Have you ever heard of the saying, "there is more than one way to skin a cat?" Well, there is more than one way to make millions in real estate.

I remember when I was first introduced to the concept of short-term rentals in 2018 when an 18-year-old student of mine changed my life and shifted my thinking. He was living in Florida while I was transitioning from Texas, and one day he exposed me to short-term rentals and the process I teach today. I was familiar with Airbnb, but I did not know much about making money with it. In 2018, I was handling my real estate business the traditional way. I was buying and flipping, expanding my rental portfolio with over 42 properties at the time, and I was so naive as to how short-term rentals worked. Quite honestly, it just wasn't on my radar.

My student asked me if I would invest the capital for him to rent a few apartments, and in turn, he would list them on a platform called Airbnb. The twist was that instead of renting out the properties every month with a traditional one-year or two-year lease agreement, he would furnish them with the home's necessities and provide the amenities for a comfortable home away from home. He went on further to say that he would rent the properties out nightly. At that time, the average rate per night was approximately $120 for a one-bedroom apartment. It sounded like a win-win situation, so I told him I would invest. It was a modest investment, and with the money, he leased five apartments. To my surprise, within three months, he had already made the original investment and was making more money on one unit than I was driving in my properties with my long-term tenants.

My mind was blown. It was at that moment I started to evaluate how I was operating my business. It opened my eyes to an easier way, with less liability, to earn profits in real estate. I was profiting approximately $300 a month for my empty rental properties that I was renting out on an annual basis. Meanwhile, he was making anywhere from $1,000 to $1,500 profit per month on each one-bedroom apartment that he rented.

It was a lightbulb moment. What I learned in that teachable moment was I did not need an expansive real estate portfolio or many properties to be profitable. I also realized that I didn't have to own the properties and take on the risks of a mortgage and home expenses. This meant I could earn even more money without all of the headaches that can come along with long-term renters. My student changed the trajectory of my real estate business, and I am so glad I took the chance and said 'yes.' Today, I proudly can say I have mastered short-term rentals, and it's time to share my secrets with you.

I believe that this is a business that anyone can be profitable if they practice the methods I will be sharing throughout this book. And just like any other real estate venture, the person who is the most profitable is the person who understands the needs of the marketplace. One of the things that you will hear me teach over and over like a broken record is that you need to be a solution to someone's problem. In real estate, this can be easy if you know where to look and how to connect with those whose problems you solve. If you can locate people who are behind on their mortgage payment, or they have difficult tenants, going through a divorce, bankruptcy, or relocating, these can become prime properties for creating solutions. These properties are ideal to use for your BNB business without taking on the risks of being the property owner. Through Rental Arbitrage, you can start taking over these properties and rent them in a matter of minutes.

Now, you may wonder, what would cause a property owner or a landlord to partner with you and allow you to list their property on Airbnb? The answer to your question is many landlords, especially private people that are having property issues in this current economy, have an open mind, and their main concern is meeting their mortgage payment. They are open to exploring new avenues, and as long as you are willing to guarantee them the rent, they are likely to contract with you. But remember, there is a guarantee and commitment you must be willing to make. Once you can secure that guarantee, renting someone else's property is a good place to start and is the easiest way to get started with BNB and start making profits immediately.

The home-sharing economy has changed the world of real estate and has made it easy for anyone to enter the market. The demand for short-term rentals is at an all-time high, and many people are booking their overnight accommodations through Airbnb. Over 3 million nights are booked every single day on their website. The demand for property on Airbnb is so high that it is currently exceeding the supply. After you read this book, I want you to get started immediately. I just mentioned that over 3 million nights are booked through Airbnb's website. You can be a part of that number and start getting paid. Here is some additional information you may find useful.

Statistics on Airbnb

No matter where you live in the world, you can take part in the short-term rental business.

1. USA: $33.8 billion
2. France: $10.8 billion
3. Spain: $6.9 billion
4. Italy: $6.4 billion
5. UK: $5.6 billion
6. Australia: $4.4 billion
7. Canada: $4.3 billion
8. Japan: $3.5 billion
9. Mexico: $2.7 billion
10. Portugal: $2.3 billion

"Today, it has over 150 million users and hosts more than half a billion guests per year. Here's a look at its user base and Airbnb demographics.

- Airbnb has 5.6 million active listings worldwide.
- There are at least 100,000 cities with active Airbnb listings.
- 150 million people use Airbnb to book vacation stays or experiences.
- Over 800 million guests have stayed at Airbnbs.
- Airbnb has listings in more than 200 countries and regions."[1]

---
[1] "Airbnb Statistics and Host Insights", Insurance Zebra, 2021 https://www.google.com/url?q=https://www.airbnb.com/help/article/376/what-legal-and-regulatory-issues-should-i-consider-before-hosting-on-airbnb&sa=D&source=editors&ust=1633713541720000&usg=AOvVaw24KHxInr8piINzBLS39dxF (accessed September 1, 2021)

How Airbnb Started

Airbnb co-founders Joe Gebbia and Brian Chesky started as two cash-strapped roommates in San Francisco in 2007. To cover their rent, they rented two rooms in their apartment to visiting designers from the International Design Conference after hotels in the area were booked up. Essentially, the co-founders used an air mattress along with other essentials such as including breakfast in their apartment deals and then started renting it out. Guests were paying $80 a night to stay on this air mattress because hotels in that area were very expensive. Before they knew it, they had made enough money to cover their rent, just by renting out their air mattress. In less than ten years, their franchise, which started simply as communicating the idea via email, was worth over $25 billion! *Can you imagine that?* They realized they were on to something big, so they approached their friends in the San Francisco area about joining them on this venture, and this was the birth of Airbnb. Today the company is publicly traded and valued at about $75 billion. This story is significant for a few reasons. The first is to show you how profitable this business can be for you. The second is to show you can rent out a room that doesn't have to be an entire apartment or an entire house and that you can make money just by controlling rooms or dividing properties up into rooms.

How Does it Work?

In the short-term rental business, everyday people can showcase their personal property on Airbnb's website. Airbnb works as an intermediary between the person listing their home and the person looking to rent their home. The platform is a no-cost way for you to post your properties, and it's a great opportunity to make an additional stream of income. This is an ingenious way to make huge profits when you think about it.

The Concept

With short-term rentals, you have the option of listing a room, or you can list the entire home as a vacation rental. Take for example, that you have a two-bedroom property, with an upstairs and downstairs area and a finished basement. With the home-sharing model, you can rent out the finished basement only and make anywhere from $100- $200 a night. Or you can rent out one of the bedrooms. In other words, you don't need to rent out the entire house, and you can still make a good profit. I have students profiting thousands of dollars per month using this model. What I love about the short-term rental model is there is a constant flow of traffic to rent your place. Almost any type of property works in this model because it works like the hotel industry model. They make their profits by renting out rooms per night.

One of the benefits of short-term rentals is that you remain in control of your property. You determine the availability, the pricing, the restrictions of the rental, and more. With Airbnb, you get to determine what you will allow in your property by setting your House Rules. When using your property, you can be comforted in knowing the tenant will need to abide by the rules that you set.

Another benefit is the flexibility to host whenever you want. With the short-term rental platforms, there are no limitations to how many nights can be booked. There's no minimum or mandatory time you have to host, and you can block off dates when your property is not available. You can also set rules about your availability, how far in the future guests can book, and any advance notices needed before booking. You get to set the time when the guest will arrive and when they will check out. Additionally, you control the amount of money you will make by choosing your nightly prices, any specials, and weekly rates. You can also easily add custom details like cleaning fees, weekly discounts, and special prices for specific times of the year. You are the owner and property manager too. It's a business model that allows you to be in control. You can work when you want or close your rental when you want to take some time off to travel or spend time with your family. You can choose to personally manage, or you can have someone else manage it for you.

Airbnb Rental Arbitrage

Airbnb has become one of the major and trusted partners in the short-term rental market. They are beneficial for both the host (the person listing their property) and the guest (the person renting the property). Airbnb works as a trusted intermediary between both the host and the guests. The host can feel confident by working through Airbnb as there is a sense of security. Having Airbnb host your property allows you to trust that guests won't destroy your property without penalty. Airbnb puts the necessary insurance such as property damage insurance in place, and they vet the guests. Additionally, the website is free to use and will only take a percentage of your earnings. What I like most about this model is they have created a way for everyone to win.

A misconception that many people have about the short-term rental business is that you must own the property you list on Airbnb. One way around the risks of buying and having a mortgage is with rental arbitrage. Rental arbitrage takes an already rented property and puts it on a short-term rental site such as Airbnb. This one strategy allows you to build a massive cash flow without the stress and challenges of homeownership.

Let me explain how Airbnb rental arbitrage works. Let's say you rent an apartment for $1,600 per month from a community or a personal landlord, and you list that same apartment on Airbnb for $150 per night. An average night would get you around $3,300 on the low end. This is what I love about this model, and it's completely legal. I use this model on apartments, furnished townhomes, single-family houses, and more.

You'll learn more about these strategies as you read through this book. Taking the time to learn about short-term rentals is a good first step, however, as you continue to learn more about this market, I want you to expand your mind to see yourself earning huge profits with your rentals. After you envision your success I want you to immediately get into action.

Visit BNBRiches.com to get access to my course that will teach you more secrets on how to make money with short-term rentals along with FREE weekly training calls included. Use code "50OFF" for huge savings!

CHAPTER TWO
GETTING STARTED-
THE BEGINNING STEPS

Before we dive into the 'how-tos' of making money with your short-term rental property, I want to first discuss the importance of creating a business entity so that you can reap the most benefits. The short-term business is no different than any other business in that you will need to have a plan. You will need to set goals on the income you want to make, the clients you want to serve, incorporate your legal business structure, purchase insurance, build your team, implement your system, and be familiar with any regulations in the city you want to have properties located. You must envision and plan for success.

The foundation to any healthy business is a solid plan. In fact, I have found that having a proper business structure in place has allowed me to expand my short-term rental business in a short period of time. The truth is many more opportunities are available if you have your business set up properly. In my past books and YouTube videos, I detailed how to set up a business with step-by-step instructions, so if you haven't set up your business yet, please reference those resources.

Just as an overview, you'll need to have a business established with:

1. Either a LLC, S- Corporation, or C-Corporation
2. An Employee Identification Number (EIN)
3. A professional online presence with a professional website, a professional phone number, and a professional email.

I am also an advocate of securing business lines of credit to help you grow and fund your business faster.

GETTING STARTED- THE BEGINNING STEPS

Be sure to get copies of my past books that talk about this and offer the resources to build your business credit. Your business setup is paramount. Trust me on this; you want your business to appear credible. This will come into play when you start searching for your properties through apartment owners and landlords. Property owners will want to do business with other business owners and they'll feel more comfortable when you have a business plan, you're able to protect their property, and you can provide them the benefit of guaranteed rents.

Because I have a business set up properly, I am able to approach apartment complexes and set up corporate leases and rent multiple units on one property. Can you imagine how much easier this has made things in my business? Instead of making money with just one unit, I am able to make more money by having multiple units and save my team the hassle of running around to multiple complexes because we have multiple properties on-site. I am able to do this through corporate leases. I can't say it enough, setting up your business will set you apart from your competitors.

Before you begin your business, you will need to do your due diligence and research short-term rentals in the areas you will have properties. You'll need to check for any regulations and restrictions. You will operate an ethical business which means you must abide by the city regulations.

"Some cities have laws that restrict your ability to host paying guests for short periods. These laws are often part of a city's zoning or administrative codes. In many cities, you must register, get a permit, or obtain a license before you list your property or accept guests. Certain types of short-term bookings may be prohibited altogether. Local governments vary greatly in how they enforce these laws. Penalties may include fines or other enforcement.

"In some tax jurisdictions, Airbnb will take care of calculating, collecting, and remitting local occupancy tax on your behalf. Occupancy tax is calculated differently in every jurisdiction. In the meantime, please review your local laws before listing your space on Airbnb."[2] As a business owner, you are responsible for knowing and adhering to the regulations in your city. When deciding whether to become an Airbnb host, you need to understand how the laws work in your city or the city you will be hosting.

On the Airbnb website, you can find hosting regulations in the United States by visiting:

https://www.airbnb.com/help/article/1376/responsible-hosting-in-the-united-states

To begin our journey together, I am providing you with a checklist at the end of this chapter to help you start your Airbnb business. You'll learn more about these steps as you work through this book. Now that you have had an overview in the next few chapters, we will go deeper into finding properties, price them and list them.

---

[2] "What legal and regulatory issues should I consider before hosting on Airbnb?", Airbnb Inc., October 30, 2020 https://www.airbnb.com/help/article/376/what-legal-and-regulatory-issues-should-i-consider-before-hosting-on-airbnb (accessed September 1, 2021)

GETTING STARTED - THE BEGINNING STEPS

Checklist: How to Start an Airbnb Business

1. Planning

- ☐ Check Airbnb Regulations in Your Area
- ☐ Financial Viability
- ☐ Suitability
- ☐ Identify The Processes

2. Setup

- ☐ Furnish The Property
- ☐ Get Photographs
- ☐ Create Airbnb Listing
- ☐ Setup Key Hand Over Process
- ☐ Get Home Emergency Cover
- ☐ Ensure Property Is Fire safe
- ☐ Setup Cleaning Team
- ☐ Linen Service
- ☐ On-call Handyman & Locksmith
- ☐ Prepare Cleaning Checklist* (included)
- ☐ Setup Payment Process

3. Operations
- ☐ Guest Communication
- ☐ Arrange Cleaning
- ☐ Manage Check-in/Check out
- ☐ Troubleshooting

4. Maintenance
- ☐ Regular Cleaning Checks
- ☐ Keep Supplies Topped Up
- ☐ Improvement Based on Guest Reviews

Visit BNBRiches.com to get access to my course that will teach you more secrets on how to make money with short-term rentals along with FREE weekly training calls included. Use code "50OFF" for huge savings!

CHAPTER THREE
FINDING THE PERFECT PROPERTY

Securing your property is the next step in building your million-dollar business. Having the right-fit property is an essential asset to your new business. Do you know that you can be profitable with any type of property when it comes to the short-term rental business model? Many people immediately think that for a property to be profitable, it needs to be near the beach, the lake, or a Caribbean Island. They believe that a property near a monument or historic landmark like the Eiffel Tower is needed in order for people to want to rent the property, but that's just not the truth. In the short-term rental business, every type of property is a fair game. The keyword is property. I have found success with very typical or everyday types of properties. Properties can include rooms, a condo, a pool house, or a guest house. Do you know you can even rent out a Windstream, the van with the bathroom and the little bed? Yes, that is right, those are considered properties also. You can check out Airbnb, VRBO, and HomeAway and see the types of properties they are listing. Think about this for a moment. How many potentially good properties have you passed over because you didn't look at them from this perspective? How many potentially good properties have you passed over because you didn't think it was fancy enough for people to rent? I hope you now have a different perspective on this.

Properties to Rent

You can rent entire places on Airbnb, such as homes and mansions, private rooms, shared rooms, and even hotel rooms. Both traditional properties and quirky listings perform well on the site, as social media and

Airbnb's wanderlust factor have inspired many to book outside-of-the-box travel experiences.

Traditional Properties include:
- Houses
- Bed and breakfasts
- Apartments
- Bungalows
- Guest suites
- Lofts
- Villas
- Pool Houses

Non-Traditional Properties include:
- Cabins
- Farms
- Tiny homes
- Boats

Now that you have had a moment to look at the wide array of properties you can list, I want you to decide on the type of properties you want to list. Will you go after properties that are entire homes? Will you focus on condos? Do you want to rent out apartments? Decide on what niche you want to focus on.

I am sure you are probably wondering by now, how do you find the properties and who you should target for your properties? Those are very good questions. The first thing you will need to do is decide on the location of your property. From there, you will approach property owners that will include private landlords and apartment complexes. I want to share some tips with you to accomplish this easily. Finding the locations and tenants can be easily done once you learn and practice the concepts.

Decide on the Location

Think about where you want your properties to be located. This is important to decide as soon as possible because at the beginning of your business operations, you will most likely be the one doing the day-to-day upkeep and servicing of your properties, and it would be easier to work from a location close in proximity to you. You want to look for a location that is convenient to you with easy access when you are starting. As you grow your business and hire team members, you can spread out your property proximity and even rent properties in different states and countries but to start; it's a good rule to keep your properties close.

Create Your Property Criteria

When looking for a location, consider one that is located in a good community. The residence should be nice and clean, and aesthetically pleasing. It should be appealing for guests traveling and looking for short and long-term stays. As you are considering properties, think about your ideal target clientele. Personally, I like to target professional guests like lawyers, doctors, engineers, and business owners. They are constantly traveling and looking for a good place to stay. They don't mind spending a little extra to be comfortable, and generally, they are not looking to host a wild weekend party. I have found professionals to be more conscious about taking care of the properties they lease. Keeping with these professional parameters has been how we make big money in our business.

When considering properties, look for a property with great amenities. Professionals like host homes that have stainless steel appliances, community or private pools, and gyms. Having a nearby shopping center and an easy commute to the highway are also good selling points. Consider a location that is centrally located or has easily sellable features. Think about what is essential in a property for your future tenant and find locations that match your criteria. Another rule of thumb is to look for properties that you would not have an issue staying in. If it's good enough for you, it will be good for your guest.

Search for Property Owners

After you identify the ideal neighborhoods, your next step is to find the property owners with properties in those areas. Throughout this process, keep in mind that you are bringing solutions. Think about who ideally would be a candidate with properties that are having problems finding tenants or keeping up with the property management. The easiest ones to start with are landlords. You want owners who already have a property that they rent out to long-term tenants. That is going to be the easiest person by far to contact to start your Airbnb business. Let me also add this. Although I am teaching you how to build a six and seven-figure business with your short-term rentals, I don't want you to start with the apartment complexes just yet. I want you to master getting your properties from private sellers, tired landlords, or just homeowners looking to lease their property.

Locating property owners is pretty easy. You can find them on Craigslist. You can also find them on websites like, For rent by owner (www.forrentbyowner.com). If you Google rent by owner, tons of different private websites will pop up where typical everyday landlords have listed their properties for rent. A few others are Zillow (www.zillow.com) and Trulia (www.trulia.com). These sites have features where private homeowners list their properties either for sale or for rent. Hotpads (www.hotpads.com) is another resource for properties. I like these websites because any person that is listing their properties there has raised their hand and indicated they're looking for a tenant. They are also willing to go the non-conventional way of finding a tenant. My students also find them by using bandit signs. Yes; bandit signs still do work. My students are finding great properties by driving in their cars, contacting the owners, and sealing the deal. I know this seems like the old way of real estate but trust me, this works. A bandit sign is another potential property waving at you.

Once you make your list of potential properties, prepare to reach out and inquire about the property. You're going to contact the person listing the property just as if you are a regular tenant inquiring. After you connect with the landlord, you will make an appointment for a site visit. During your first call and site visit, you will not disclose any information to them just yet. You will have a more in-depth conversation with them after you decide you want to move forward with the property. I would also suggest that you don't introduce yourself as a business owner just yet. You don't want to send up any red flags before you have had the opportunity to pitch your proposal. If the property owner is not aware of how working with a professional property management company can work or benefit them, they will probably be hesitant to meet with you. And quite frankly, you don't know just yet if this property is a good fit for Airbnb. So, before you disclose too much, make sure it is a property you are truly interested in. You need to ensure that it meets your criteria and it will be a good property for your professional tenants.

After you have conducted your site visit and have decided the location is a good match for your property criteria, you are ready to move forward. The next step is to propose your offer to the property owner. Now don't allow this part to intimidate you because this is where many people get stuck. Talking to the property owner is the fun part and what you will spend most of your time doing when you first get started. Get familiar with the script that I have provided in this chapter so that you can become proficient and comfortable with the pitch. The script works, and the success my students are having is proof. I personally use the script with NuuRez. I want you to learn it so you can go out into the world and start implementing this and making money. If you follow along with the script, it will make it so much easier to close the deal.

Your pitch or offer will be done after you leave the property. You don't want to do this face to face when you are first getting started. Selling is an art form. And if you have not perfected the art just yet, having the conversation over the phone will allow you the opportunity to gather yourself and maintain your composure. Trust me on this. You don't want to lose the deal because you seem nervous and you can't remember what to say next. Utilize the script. When you speak with the owner you're going to convince them to allow you to lease their property and host it on Airbnb or whatever site you choose. This is both legal and ethical if you have full disclosure.

When talking with these property owners, you will convince them that you are the right fit for their property, and you are the tenant they want. In your pitch, you want to highlight your experience and what it is that you offer. With the script at the end of this chapter, you will find it easy to speak with them once you have everything in place. You will convince them that you are an awesome and easy decision for them to make.

From there, you will sell the benefits of them choosing you. Sell them on the benefits of working with you and how easy you will make things for them. If they ask you what your company does, share with them who you serve. Let them know that you serve professionals. Let them know you provide safe, clean, and comfortable accommodations for your clients, many of whom want to stay in accommodations at great facilities with great amenities while they are traveling. You do not need to go into details about what type of professionals you serve. Ultimately you want them to be convinced that working with you will not only guarantee their rent; it will also expose their property to your network of professionals, which will result in repeat rentals. You are also offering them a property management service free of charge that will host short-term vacationers and corporate professionals into the property.

The benefits are what will set you apart from others in the marketplace. This may seem like an overemphasis but think of it this way. If they have had problems with tenants in the past, they may be skeptical about how this will work for them. But, although they may have had issues with tenants before, you are the solution. You are the tenant that is going to be able to pay the rent. You can also emphasize the benefits of listing their properties on Airbnb, including the $1M protection for property damage and 24/7 global service.

In addition, you offer additional benefits such as:

- You will maintain the property and keep it in like-new condition and in for sale condition.
- The property will be professionally photographed.
- You will decorate and furnish the apartment.
- Guaranteed rents.
- Free Property Management services. If anything goes wrong with the property, you will be responsible for fixing it.
- Insurance for the property.
- Optional: Revenue sharing. (See the next section for additional information)

Some property owners may need a bit more convincing, and that's okay and not necessarily a red flag. They may not be familiar with how an Airbnb model will work or think that it will be too much required on their end. If they need a bit more persuading, you can show them your ability to guarantee the rents, and that can be shown through your credit cards, or whatever it is that you have at least enough money to pay the rent. If you need assistance in this area, you can get connected to our group as well. We have access to funding; at NuuRez we help our students in this area, especially for those that are just starting in the business.

Revenue Sharing

As a last resort option for closing the deal is revenue sharing. With this option, you can offer to give the owner a percentage of the money that you make on top of the rent that you're paying them. This is not an option that I suggest you lead with because you are cutting into your profit, but if you're up against a tough owner and you really want the property, offering a revenue sharing option will be the big fish to close the deal. With this option, not only are they receiving a long-term lease with guaranteed rent, a maintained property, you are also giving them a portion of your revenue. That is a win-win! Now, if you are winning before you offer the revenue share, don't offer this. If you are new to the business, this might help you close more deals quicker.

Closing the Deal

When they are ready to proceed, you will sign their standard lease along with a lease addendum or co-hosting Agreement. The best and preferred option of these is the Lease Addendum. The standard lease terms usually consist of formalities about no subletting and other restrictions. This is fine for you to sign along with the addendum.

Lease Addendum

The addendum that you will have them sign negates some of those formalities and states that the property owner agrees to allow clients to stay in your property. The lease addendum allows you to place the property on Airbnb, and they can view it.

Co-Hosting Agreement

The second type of agreement is a co-hosting agreement. Co-hosts help listing owners take care of their homes and guests. It can be profitable for you because you will enter into a management agreement that allows you to receive property management fees.

The ideal candidate for a co-hosting agreement is a property owner that may just have one unit on Airbnb. Moreover, you can charge those management fees directly to the person via Airbnb by adding that in as an additional fee.

Corporate Leases

Corporate leases have been a huge game-changer for me and a secret that I share with my students. Corporate leasing is when you rent apartments, multi-units, and properties in your business name. You will need to have a few things in place for corporate leasing. The obvious for a corporate lease is you must have your business in place. I know I have probably overemphasized this, but in order to really grow and scale and oversee multiple properties, this is a requirement. There are many apartment complexes, private landlords, and property owners that will rent their property to your business that would not normally consider leasing to an individual.

Allow me to recap the steps for you one more time to ensure you are clear on the process.

- Step #1: Make an appointment with the owner.
- Step #2: Visit the property. Ask the questions you need to know, i.e., Rent amount, past tenants. Be engaging in the conversation.
- Step #3: Call back to discuss the contract after the appointment. Do not discuss what you will be offering at the initial meeting.
- Step #4: Pitch your offer and sell the benefits.
- Step #5: Close the deal.

Visit BNBRiches.com to get access to my course that will teach you more secrets on how to make money with short-term rentals along with FREE weekly training calls included. Use code "50OFF" for huge savings!

NOELLE RANDALL
COACHING

Hello [OWNER/LANDLORD NAME],

[OUR COMPANY NAME] is expanding and looking for properties to rent for short term rental clients. We are looking for homeowners and landlords to partner with for corporate relocation clients, traveling clients such as nurses, doctors, sales professionals, flight attendants, pilots and so forth. We currently have locations in Alabama, Texas and Mississippi. We will manage the property so that you don't have to. It will not cost you extra, like some Management companies charge, as we are paid by our clients.

*You are guaranteed the agreed upon rent in the contract regardless, if our clients are occupying the unit or not.

All our clients are screened ahead of time and we provide cleaning services free of charge. We will also provide $1,000,000 in property damage insurance as well as $1,000,000 in liability insurance should a claim be bought against the host. Either way you are protected, and insured should anything happen. Wireless security systems will be provided at the premises to monitor the safety of the unit.

What we are looking for:

We prefer long term partnerships (1yr+)

Preferably single-family homes, condos, townhomes, and rooms in [CITY/COUNTY NAME], [LOCAL AIRPORT], [MAJOR ATTRACTION OR MEDICAL CENTER] in [NAME OF METROPLEX] area

and [OPTIONAL-OTHER MAJOR AREA OF CITY] area. We will consider other areas. We prefer safe and clean neighborhoods, as our clients are frequent travelers.

Must be close to public transportation

Please note if the property or room is not furnished. We can furnish it if it isn't.

No Pets: Generally, we do not allow pets in our properties, unless we have your expressed consent with additional compensation paid to you (property owner)

*If you are interested in your property or room being considered for our corporate partnership please go to [INSERT WEBSITE] or contact [CONTACT NAME] AT [INSERT PHONE NUMBER] for more information

Thank You!

FINDING THE PERFECT PROPERTY

Co-Hosting Agreement

This agreement is between:

[Management Company or Host Name], [Address] (referred to as "Host", or "NAME OF THE INDIVIDUAL")

AND

[Insert name of property owner], [Insert permanent Address] (referred to as "you")

1. Introduction:

This agreement sets out the terms and conditions upon which [HOST NAME] will provide short let management services to you in relation to your property that you wish to let out through Airbnb or similar homestay booking websites.

2. Definitions:

In this agreement, some terms are used regularly. These are capitalized and are defined as follows:

"Availability Period" means the period for which the Property is available for receiving Guests;

"Cleaning Fee" means a fee for cleaning and preparing the property for occupation by a Guest;

"Excluded Services" means the services that Host does not provide as part of this agreement. These are listed in Appendix A;

"Extra Maintenance Services" means services such as deep clean, carpet shampoo, upholstery cleaning, mold removal, pest control, oven cleaning, external window/balcony cleaning, wall painting, work at height, serious plumbing, electrical or gas works, and anything that is not covered by our Services;

"Fee" means the fees charged by [HOST NAME] in accordance with clause 8 below; "Guest" means a guest who is renting the property through one of the Homestay Websites;

"Homestay Website" means a short stay rental marketplace including but no allowed limited to Airbnb, Homeaway, Booking.com, FlipKey, HomeAway, and such other websites as chosen by us. In cases where a guest makes a reservation directly with the Host, [HOST NAME] will extend the concept of Homestay Website to that reservation;

"Services" means the short let management services described in clause 3 below; "Listing" means any advertisement of your Property on the Homestay Website; "Room Rent" shall mean the total amount paid by the Guest for a booking less any Airbnb Cleaning Fee and any service fee and taxes levied by the relevant Homestay Website and/or any card processing fee ;

"Property" means [property address] or such other property as agreed between [HOST NAME] and you from time to time.

3. Services

3.1 In exchange for the fee you pay to the [HOST NAME], Host shall provide the following services to you:

3.1.1 Writing up your listing and optimizing it across various Homestay Websites. The host shall select the

Homestay Websites to list on unless you tell us otherwise;

3.1.2 Managing the pricing and availability calendar across various Homestay Website(s) as Host deems fit. You agree that [HOST NAME] has the expertise to make pricing decisions and is therefore not required to consult with you before accepting a booking from a Guest or setting the price for any Bookings. However, the Host will bear in mind your requirements you have informed about your monthly income expectations or your preferences around the type of Guests you wish to accept in the property;

3.1.3 Engaging a photographer (extra fees apply) to take photos of the Property for one full photoshoot. Should you cancel or postpone this photoshoot with less than 48 hours' notice, or should a re-take photo is required due to the property not being reasonably ready as discussed, the photographer reserves the right to charge the Host an additional XX fee to cover the cost of an additional photoshoot;

3.1.4 Responding to any enquiries raised by Guests in relation to your Listings and managing all communications with the Guests including any disputes that may arise;

3.1.5 Provide housekeeping and linen service only once at the start of each Guest's stay;

3.1.6 Remotely coordinating urgent repairs or maintenance works to your property if and only if required to ensure complete Guest satisfaction; and

3.2 You agree that Host shall not provide the Excluded Services as part of this agreement. If you need any services, Host can discuss them as and when needed and agree to arrange them for you for extra cost plus our expenses.

4. Host Obligations

4.1 In order to allow us to provide the Services set out in this agreement you agree that Owner will:

4.1.1 Provide us with complete, accurate and timely information about the Property and any other information reasonably requested by us. It is your responsibility to ensure that we have all the information needed to operate and maintain the Property and look after the safety of each Guest;

4.1.2 Provide all the items set out in essentials checklist (see Appendix B). If these are not provided, we will buy these and charge you at cost plus reasonable expenses;

4.1.3 Maintain the Property at all times which includes doing repairs as soon as possible upon request by [Host Name] or refunding [Host Name] for any repairs;

4.1.4 Comply with all legal requirements applicable to a landlord in the US including but not limited to fire safety regulations, gas and electrical safety, etc.;

4.1.5 Remove or lock away any expensive and fragile items in the Property and let us know about any particularly fragile or sensitive areas in the Property that you want us to bear in mind;

4.1.6 Empty at all shelf in the fridge, kitchen cabinets, and in the bathroom and at least 1 drawer in a wardrobe for Guest use; and

4.1.7 Cooperate fully with us in the provision of the Services and pay our Fee and other costs when due.

5. Availability Period and Minimum Agreement

5.1 You will make the Properties available to us for short letting for a minimum period of 2 months, starting [ ] (the "initial Availability Period"). You may not reduce the initial Availability Period without our prior consent otherwise charges in Clause 5.2 below shall apply. You may extend the initial Availability Period by giving us notice at any time and any extension shall be as agreed between us from time to time in the initial Availability Period.

FIXED TERM OPTION

You will make the Properties available to the Host for short-term stays from [DATE] to [DATE] (the "initial Availability Period"). You may not reduce the initial Availability Period without our prior consent otherwise charges in Clause 5.2 below shall apply. You may extend the Availability 5.1 Period by giving us notice at any time and any extension shall be as agreed between us from time to time in the initial Availability Period

5.2 If you would like to terminate the agreement during the initial Availability Period, you may do so by paying a break fee of XXX in addition to the other costs and fees that may be incurred.

5.3 HOST shall charge a Fee at the rate of X% for any reservation obtained by us during the period [DATE] but which occurs after this agreement is terminated. For the avoidance of doubt, Host will not charge any Cleaning Fee for future reservations and you may retain this fee where it has been charged to the Guest.

5.4 Upon termination, Host shall return your keys on the last day of the notice period or such other date as agreed.

5.5 The Fee for Host Services provided up until the date of termination and any Fee payable as per Clause 5.3. or Clause 6.1. shall become payable immediately following termination and receipt of our final invoice.

6. Cancellation or Refunds of Bookings

6.1 If you cancel or cause a Guest to cancel any Booking or if Host is required to refund a part of a Booking, you shall be required to pay the following charges:

a. the Homestay Website's cancellation charges, if applicable;1

b. any charges levied by payment processing sites for refunds, if applicable; and

c. [Host Name]'s Fee for that booking in its entirety.

6.2 For the avoidance of doubt, "causing a Guest to cancel a Booking" shall include any situation where a Booking is cancelled due to the Property being uninhabitable due to lack of heating, hot water, plumbing, electricity, and Wi-Fi or due to gas leaks, water leaks, rodents, pests, lack of cleanliness or other such serious deficiencies.

7. Fee and Payment

7.1 Host Fees shall be X% of the Room Rent.

7.2 the Room Rent from each Guest and will go directly into your account from Homestay websites and Host will bill you on a monthly basis along with any other fees or expenses incurred by Host on your behalf from the Room Rent.

7.3 The Cleaning Fee for each Booking shall be paid directly to the cleaner. Where a Homestay Website does not have a separate provision for charging Cleaning Fees to the Guest, the Room Rent shall be adjusted so as to take into account a Cleaning Fee.

7.4 You will not be entitled to withhold by way of set-off, deduction, or counterclaim any amounts which you owe to the Homestay Website against any amounts that you owe to Host or vice versa.

7.5 You agree to pay interest on any amount payable under this agreement and not paid on the due date, for the period from the due date to the date of payment at a rate equal to X%.

8. Extra Charges

8.1 In addition to the Fee stated above, the only other extra charges that will apply are as follows:

8.2 If you choose to stay in the apartment during the Availability Period, Host will clean the apartment for you after your stay and charge you the cost of the cleaning to you unless told otherwise (see Appendix C for details);

8.3 Any emergency runner services will be charged at XX in case needed (see clause 9 on Maintenance below for details); and

8.4 Extra Maintenance Services will be charged separately but only if you ask the Host to book these for you.

9. Property Maintenance and Expenses

9.1 You agree that you shall be primarily responsible for the maintenance and upkeep of the Property and shall ensure that the Property is in a good condition for Guests' use.

9.2 You also agree and acknowledge that there will be some amount of normal wear and tear of the Property due to Guest use and that you shall be responsible for making good such wear and tear.

9.3 Ensuring positive Guest requires urgent attention to maintenance requirements. You authorize [Host Name] to incur expenses of up to XXX (for each individual event) on your behalf to conduct any emergency repairs or maintenance works or take such action which [Host Name] believes are reasonably necessary to secure a good review from a Guest.

9.4 We agree that we shall not undertake any significant or major repairs exceeding XXX without your prior express consent except under extenuating circumstances where there is a major safety hazard to life or property.

10. Liability and Other Terms

10.1 You understand and agree that [Host Name] does not act as an insurer and that you shall obtain the appropriate insurance for the Property and its contents.

10.2 You also agree and understand that Host is not providing investment advice or real estate advice and that you shall make your own independent decision on whether short lets are the right solution for you. Whilst the Host will use reasonable skill in attracting bookings, Host cannot guarantee that you will make an income of any particular amount and Host will not be responsible for lost opportunity cost or loss of earnings if you don't get any bookings for whatever reason. Nor Host is liable for the suitability of the Guests given that we rely upon the verification standards of the Homestay Website and the relevant profile pages to assess suitability.

10.3 Whilst Host will use reasonable care to identify any issues that are readily apparent from regular inspection of the Property by the Host, but Host will not be responsible for the condition, safety, or security of the Property. You, as the property owner, will be solely responsible for such conditions, safety, and security, and compliance with all laws, rules, and regulations applicable to the Property.

10.4 You will be liable to the Guest in respect of the quality, safety, and description of the Property and will also be responsible for ensuring that the Property is both available on the dates which have been booked and are in the condition as listed or described.

10.5 You agree to indemnify and hold us harmless from and against any claims, liabilities, damages, losses, and expenses including (without limitation) reasonable legal fees, arising out of, or in connection with, any breach by you of this agreement or the terms of any agreement you may have in place with the Homestay Website from time to time.

10.6 You will contract directly with a Guest and we will not be liable in respect of any matter arising which relates to a Booking between you, as Host, and a Guest which includes the breakage of any items at the property caused by the Guest or due to reasons beyond our reasonable control.

10.7 We will not be liable for the provision of services by third parties (any "Third Party Supplier"), including those who provide the Extra Maintenance Services or any other maintenance or repair services that we book on your behalf. However, we will ensure that we take reasonable care and skill in selecting such Third-Party Suppliers.

10.8 We will not be liable to you or be deemed to be in breach of this agreement by reason of any delay in performing, or any failure to perform, any of our obligations if the delay or failure was due to any cause beyond our reasonable control such as shortages, severe weather, power or other utility cut-offs, burglary, natural disaster, strikes, governmental action, terrorism, war, civil unrest or other similar occurrences.

10.9 In no event shall we be liable for exemplary, incidental, indirect, special, or consequential damages or for any business, financial or economic loss such as lost reputation, lost bargain, lost profit or loss of anticipated savings arising out of or resulting from this agreement (even if we have been advised of the possibility thereof or we are asked by the Host to act against what we believe to be their best interests) and whether such loss arises as a result of negligence, breach of this property management contract, or otherwise by us or any agent, employee or third party providing services on our behalf (including a Third Party Supplier) except to the extent the foregoing limitation is prohibited by applicable law.

10.10 Notwithstanding anything to the contrary herein, subject to any exceptions set forth in applicable law, our liability for all losses, damages, and other liabilities relating to or arising out of this agreement and the Services provided hereunder (including, without limitation, with respect to property damage, damage to valuable or fragile items at the Property, personal injury, and death) will be limited to the cost of obtaining replacement services or the average one month's Fee for our Services, whichever is the higher amount.

11. Miscellaneous

11.1 Both parties warrant that they have the power to enter into this agreement and have obtained all necessary approvals to do so.

11.2 The relationship between you and us is that of an independent contractor. We are not your agents, employees, or partner of yours. No partnership, joint venture, association, alliance, or other fiduciary, employee/employer, principal/agent or other relationship other than that of the independent contractor shall be created by this agreement, express or implied.

11.3 Each party acknowledges that these documents contain the whole agreement between the parties hereto and that it has not relied upon any oral or written representations made to it by the other or its employees or agents. Nothing in this clause shall limit or exclude any liability for fraud.

11.4 The parties agree that this agreement is fair and reasonable. However, if any provision of this agreement is held not to be valid by a court of competent jurisdiction but would be valid if part of the wording was deleted, then such provision shall apply with such deletions as may be necessary to make it valid and the remaining provisions shall remain in full force and effect and this agreement shall be enforced in such manner as carried out as closely as possible the intent of the parties hereto.

11.5 No failure or delay by us in exercising any right or remedy provided by law or under this agreement and no single or partial exercise of any such right or remedy shall impair the right or remedy, or operate as a waiver or variation of it, or preclude its exercise at any subsequent time.

11.6 This agreement and any non-contractual rights or obligations arising from or in connection with this agreement shall be governed by and construed in accordance with the laws of [INSERT JURISDICTION]. You agree, as we do, to submit to the exclusive jurisdiction of the [NAME OF STATE/COUNTRY].

By: ....

[Host Name]

Date:

This property management contract agreed and accepted by:

Name:

Date:

Appendix A Excluded Services

[Host Name] does not provide the following services as part of this agreement:

1. Deep cleans including sofa, carpet, and other upholstery cleanings
2. Co-ordinating structural or major repairs or maintenance works on the Property
3. External window washing
4. Washing walls or repainting them
5. Furniture treatment
6. Animal waste removal
7. Gardening, garden shed cleaning, patio cleaning
8. Mold and/or bio-hazardous substance removal
9. Industrial cleaning
10. The lifting of heavy furniture

11. Cleaning surfaces above arms reach
12. Cleaning of heavily soiled areas
13. Extermination (insects etc.)
14. Yard work or garage cleaning

Appendix B Guest-Ready Checklist

[Host Name] reserves the right to buy these and charge you for them.

Bedroom Essentials

- Four Pillows per bed
- One duvet per bed
- Mattress protector
- Blackout curtains
- Bedside lamps
- Space to hang/store clothes
- Hangers
- Bedroom Furnishings
- Soft furnishings – rugs, extra cushions, throw
- Thick mattress topper
- Extra quilts for emergencies
- Kitchen Facilities
- Toaster
- Kettle
- Microwave
- Dishwasher
- Large Bin with cover

Kitchen Essentials

- Basic condiments for cooking* (for e.g. olive oil, salt, pepper, balsamic vinegar, sugar, basic spices etc.)
- 2 plates, 2 bowls, 2 coffee mugs, 2 glasses, 2 wine glasses per person
- 2 forks, 2 regular spoons, 2 teaspoons, 2 knives per person
- Frying pans, saucepans, and stock-pots in basic sizes
- Ladles*
- Cutting knives and a chopping board
- Peeler
- Serving spoons
- Pair of scissors
- Living Room Essentials
- Coffee table
- TV + cable* (free view will do as well, but good to have Apple TV or Chromecast!)
- Travel adaptor

Living Room Furnishings

- Soft furnishings
- Candles
- Floor lamps
- Books
- Board / Card Games
- Bathroom Essentials
- Hairdryer

- Toilet brush
- Toothbrush holder
- Extractor fan / Dehumidifier
- Small Bin with cover
- Bathroom Furnishings
- Full-length mirror
- Toilet roll holder
- Rack or cabinet space for towels and guests' toiletries
- Shower curtains for a bathtub if necessary
- Cleaning Essentials
- Mop and Bucket
- Vacuum cleaner and one pack of bags
- Multi-surface cleaning liquid
- Dustpan & brush
- Dishwasher tablets
- Washer detergent tablets
- Dishwasher salt
- Diffuser liquid for bathrooms/room freshener
- Febreze fabric freshener
- Mold spray

Other Home Essentials

- Working Wi-fi
- Iron & Ironing Board
- Washing Machine
- Clothes Stand (Even if you have a tumble dryer!)
- Wine opener

- Bottle opener
- Extension Cord
- Extra batteries for remote controls
- Extra bulbs for lamps & ceiling down-lights with correct wattage and specs
- Carpet slippers if your home is carpeted
- Electric heaters for emergencies

CHAPTER FOUR
PREPARING YOUR PROPERTY

The preparation of your property and how you list it will be key to keeping your property filled with happy renters. And if you like to shop or decorate, this is where the fun will begin for you. When furnishing your home, you want to invest in good quality furniture that will last. Now that doesn't equate to spending thousands and tens of thousands of dollars. You can furnish homes for just a few $1,000, and you can do all of it on credit. I have purchased furniture from City Furniture, Rooms to Go, and other furniture stores. With their credit plan, I did not have to make payments for two years, which gave me plenty of time to get myself up and running before I had to make my first payment. There are creative ways to get this done, and you don't have to stress yourself trying to pay for so much upfront. You want the home to be furnished on a budget. You can find great pieces at different thrift stores, consignment stores, Salvation Army's, and Goodwill. Used furniture stores have sofas, kitchen tables, and many large furnishings you will need for the home. They often have a good assortment of décor items that can complement the home. I must add that shopping at a used store may take a bit more time to accumulate the items you need, but it is definitely worth the savings if you have the time and patience to do it.

Also, keep in mind there are certain things that you should buy new and not used, for example, a mattress. Surely, you don't want to put dirty old mattresses in your properties; this is very important. Utilize the checklist provided at the end of this chapter as you go shopping and only buy the things that you need. I have witnessed so many people overspend on furniture and accessories for the house. If you are a bargain shopper, this is a good time to use your thrifty skills to bring the home together nicely. Keep to the budget you have set for this area.

The second thing that you will need to purchase after furniture is the supplies. Supplies include your pots, pans, dishes, forks and knives, and the things that people will need if they stay at your property for an extended period. Remember, this is a short-term rental where people expect to just come with a suitcase and get everything that they need for their stay. This is pretty easy to put together. Many of the items on the checklist you can purchase directly from the dollar store. Walmart and Target are also good options for great prices. You don't have to purchase expensive items to provide a great stay for your guest.

Allow me to share some tips on how to keep your place looking crisp, clean, and appealing to your renters. I always purchase white towels and white sheets. It's one of the secrets to my Airbnbs, always having a clean and bright appeal. I know there are many people teaching others to use colorful towels and linens when stocking the home, but I don't agree with this. I have found white to be easier to wash and replace easily should they get soiled or damaged. I also think that white looks very professional, and besides, it's what the hotels use, and they have set the standard for the hospitality industry. Of course, white will get dirty easier but don't be overly concerned about the renter that may mess up the towel or linens because the house rules will indicate the penalties should the supplies be damaged.

Home Signage and Welcome Binder

Once you have furnished the home and purchased the supplies, next, you will need to make the signage for the home. Signage makes it more convenient for your guest to find what they need. You should put signage around the home that tells people how to use the washer and dryer and where to locate anything they need. You should put a sign near the toilet that tells them not to flush different things down there. You'll need signage with instructions on how to use the microwave. The key to this is convenience for the guest, and it also minimizes the need for them to contact you.

In addition to the signage, you will have a welcome book for your guests. Every good host should have a welcome binder for their guests in every property they host. The welcome book will list all pertinent information for your guest to make their stay comfortable. Your guest may have simple questions, and with your welcome binder, you're going to make sure that they are already answered. The binder will list where things are located in the house, how to operate the appliances and electronics, and how to contact you or the person you have in charge of the property should the need arise. The welcome book also outlines how the guest should do things and the house rules. It will list what time is check-in and check-out, where to find local restaurants and grocery stores, and any emergency information. Once you have your information compiled, you will place it in a binder in a place the guest can easily locate it. This doesn't have to be anything fancy. You can buy a binder from the dollar store with sheet protections for your printed pages. You can use the sample welcome letter that I have provided and make any tweaks to it to fit your needs for your binder.

Remove Items from the Home

Lastly, when preparing the property, remove all of the personal items from the home. This will be more applicable to you if you are renting out your personal home. Your guest will want a great experience similar to a hotel, and I'm not sure about you, but I have never been to a hotel room and saw someone's toothbrush in the bathroom. This is no different from your property. You don't want your Airbnb to have your stuff scattered around because it's not professional. Remove all of your personal items whenever a guest is going to be there. This includes combs, curling irons, razors, or anything that personally belongs to you. Remember you want to create a great experience for your guests, so when they are comfortable with a clean environment and the things they need are at their fingertips, they will not only give you a great review, but they will come back and stay with you again.

Visit BNBRiches.com to get access to my course that will teach you more secrets on how to make money with short-term rentals along with FREE weekly training calls included. Use code "50OFF" for huge savings!

Property Setup / Budget Expense

Room	Category	Item	Quantity
KITCHEN	Dinnerware	Plates - Large	4
		Plates - Small	4
		Bowls	4
		Glasses - Tall	4
		Glasses - Tall	4
		Coffee Cups	4
		Wine Glasses	4
		Plastic Cups	2
		Plastic Bowls	2
		Plastic Plates)	2
		Placemats	4
		3 pc Dining Set	1
	Cutlery	Silverware Set	1
		Serving spoons/forks	4
		Butcher block of knives	1
	Cookware/Bakeware	Set of pots and pans with lids	1
		Saute pans large	1
		Saute pans 1 small	1
		Cookie sheet (2)	2
		Glass/metal dish (9x13 & 9x9)	2
	Utensils	Cutting board	2
		Plastic/wood spoons	2
		Spatula	1
		Ladle	1

PREPARING YOUR PROPERTY

		Vegetable peeler	1
		Tongs	1
		Whisk	1
		Can opener	1
		Corkscrew	1
		Bottle opener	1
		Grater	1
		Measuring cups	1
		Colander	1
		Paper towel holder	1
		Paper towels	
		Utensil Tray	1
	Small appliances	Coffee Maker - Keurig	1
		Coffee, Coffee filters, sugar, cream	
		Coffee Pod Storage Tray	1
		Tea kettle	1
		Tea bags	
		Toaster	1
		Crockpot	1
	Large appliances	Refrigerator	1
		Stove	1
		Oven	1
		Microwave	1
		Dishwasher	1
	Miscellaneous	Salt and pepper	2
		Dishrag (4)	4
		Dish towel (4)	4

		Oven mitts	1
		Kitchen rug at sink	1
		Trash can	1
		Dish soap & Dishwasher pods	
LIVING ROOM	Living Area	Sofa Couch	1
		Chair	1
		Smart TV - 50 inch	1
		Lighting	1
		Coffee Table	1
		Side Tables	1
		Throw Pillow covers - set of 2	2
		Throw pillows	4
		Fake Flowers	10
		Rug	1
		TV Mount	1
		Curtains	2
		Painting	1
	Dining Area	Table	1
		Chairs	2
		Lighting	1
	OFFICE	Office Desk	1
		Office Chair	1
KING BEDROOM	Bedding	Mattress	1
		Box Spring	1
		Bed Frame	1
		Mattress cover	1
		Sheets Sets	2

PREPARING YOUR PROPERTY

		Extra Pillows - 6	3
		Extra Pillowcases - 12 pack	1
		Comforter	1
		Curtains	2
		3pc Duvet Cover Set	1
	Furn/Elec	Nightstand beside bed	1
		Alarm Clock	1
		Smart TV-32 inch	1
		Full body mirror	1
		TV Mount	1
		Painting	1
	Closet	Hangers 10 pack	2
		Iron	1
		Iron Board Cover	1
		Iron Hanger	1
		Extra blanket	1
BATHROOM	Linens	Bath towels	4
		Hand towels	4
		Wash cloths	4
		Makeup Rags - pack of 12	1
		Bathmat Set	1
	Decor	Shower curtain	
		Shower liner	1
		Shower rod and rings	
		Wastebasket	1
		Hairdryer	1
		Toilet Brush	1

		Toilet plunger	1
		Bathroom Accessories Set	1
		Shower Dispensor	
		Toilet Tissue	
Other		Heating/Air conditioning	
		Smoke and CO detector	
		Vacuum cleaner	1
		Mop & bucket	1
		Broom	1
		First Aid Kit	1
		Simple dedcorative pieces	1
GARAGE/ GAME ROOM			
Extras			
		Wi-Fi	
		Board games?	
		Streaming device	
		Welcome gift for guest?	
		Combat Roach Bait	1

PREPARING YOUR PROPERTY

CLEANING CHECKLIST

CHANGE LINEN & TOWELS

- ☐ Strip used linen, bed sheets, towels, bathmats and tea towels. Replace with fresh.
- ☐ Extra set- Bed linen, blanket, sheets, pillow case, and towels are fresh & clean.

CLEAN KITCHEN

- ☐ Wash and put away any dishes left out
- ☐ Empty dishwasher (please make sure dishes are dry)
- ☐ Clean fridge – remove anything left behind by guests, wipe any spills,
- ☐ Empty and clean stove/oven
- ☐ Empty and clean Microwave
- ☐ Make sure other appliances are empty and clean
- ☐ Clean surfaces, wipe down kitchen counter, bar area, chairs and benches
- ☐ Clean and polish sink, taps and other hardware
- ☐ Sweep, mop and/or vacuum floors/rugs
- ☐ Empty trash bins and replace trash bag(make sure wall and area near trash bin is clean and free of food debri)

CLEAN BATHROOM

- ☐ Sanitize and clean toilet
- ☐ Clean and shine sink and mirrors

- ☐ Scrub clean shower
- ☐ Clean glass shower door/ curtains and make sure it is free of grime (replace or wash curtains and liners that are very dirty)
- ☐ Check bath rugs/mats (wash them if they are stained)
- ☐ Don't forget to check drain holes.
- ☐ Empty trash bins and replace trash bag

Living Room / Bedroom(s)

- ☐ Beds clean and properly made
- ☐ Clear under beds and sofas
- ☐ Areas wiped down and free of dust (electronics, tables, furniture, surfaces, light switches and skirting boards)
- ☐ Electronics/outlets are working (all T.V. has remotes).
- ☐ Make sure all lights are working (keep some spare light bulbs handy!),
- ☐ Taps aren't dripping or leaking,
- ☐ Tans, air conditioning and heaters work
- ☐ Check tidiness / cleanliness of cushions, rugs, and decor items.
- ☐ Floor swept, mopped or vacuumed.
- ☐ Check that guests haven't left anything behind.

RE-STOCK CONSUMABLES

- ☐ Make sure to refill supplies such as: tea, coffee, sugar, creamer, paper towel, bin liners, cling/foil wrap, dish soap, sponges, facial tissues, toilet paper, hand soap, shampoo, conditioner, body wash, laundry liquids/pods etc.

Dust, Tidy, Reset

- ☐ Spot dusting throughout: wipe down tables, surfaces, light switches and skirting boards where needed. While you're doing the dusting, check that guests haven't left anything behind.
- ☐ Make sure all lights are working (keep some spare light bulbs handy!), taps aren't dripping or leaking, fans, air conditioning and heaters work and maybe keep a lamp on for your late check-in guests.
- ☐ Tidy & reset: stack magazines, plump up cushions, straighten rugs, arrange decor items, leave out guest information booklets, redraw blinds and curtains

Sweep, vacuum and mop

- ☐ Please make sure all floors are swept, mopped and/or vacuumed.
- ☐ If you have any outdoor areas, sweep up dirt, debris, leaves etc and wipe outdoor chairs so your porches, balconies and outdoor entertaining areas are neat and tidy, and dirt isn't tracked into the house. (Wipe off and bring in chair cushions if weather is rainy & store in closet)

Guest ready finishing touches

- ☐ This might include any extra touches you leave for your guests, complimentary snacks, popcorn and bottled water(2 bottles), brochures, coupons or vouchers.
- ☐ If you have a welcome board, get that set up with the guests' names.
- ☐ Check keys are returned and ready.

Welcome Letter

Hello XXXX,

We look forward to hosting you XXX-XXX and we want your stay to be 5-star. Our home is fully equipped, clean and stocked with all of your hospitality needs. Here are the check-in details (this message will also be emailed to the email on file):

Address: 123 Main St. City, State, Zip

Lockbox Code: 1234

Check-in time is 3 pm CST on the first day of your reservation. There is a lockbox on the door, you will enter the code above and retrieve the key. Please use the key to unlock the door and you will be responsible to return the door key to the lockbox at the end of your stay. Please note, there is a $250 fee for any lost keys.

When you enter the home, there is a place for the keys to be placed. You will also find a welcome book with full instructions to guide you, as well as helpful tips, resources and discounts on local activities.

If there are any issues during your stay, please call 555-123-4567.

Again, we look forward to hosting you.

NAME

COMPANY NAME

PREPARING YOUR PROPERTY

Dear [GUEST],

It would be my pleasure to welcome you from [INSERT DATE OF RESERVATION] at my [HOME/ROOM/APARTMENT] in [CITY NAME].

- *For non-emergency queries, please message us on Airbnb and we will respond as soon as possible.*
- *For an emergency during your stay, please keep my mobile number XXXXXXXXX handy at all times.*

—————Sample Airbnb welcome message—————

ACCESS INSTRUCTIONS:

Check-in time starts from 3 PM [TIME ZONE] and you are welcome to check-in anytime after that.

IF YOU ARRIVE EARLY:

If you reach here early, you are welcome to drop your luggage anytime after 11 PM and come back to check-in after 3 PM while housekeeping prepares the place for you.

OR [PLEASE REFRAIN FROM ARRIVING EARLY TO THE PROPERTY]

KEY COLLECTION

You must have received a six-digit access code (via email) immediately after you booked on Airbnb (email subject: Edinburgh Airbnb Flat Access Instructions) which will be valid for the duration of your stay. You will need to key-in your code followed by # key to unlock the door, example 123456#

To open the door, enter the above access code followed by the "#" key.

Please turn the lever "up" to unlock, please use this code to open the door first time, and you will find the keys inside to use after that.

————Sample Airbnb welcome message————

WIFI DETAILS:

Wi-Fi Network Name: TALKTALKXXXXX

Wi-Fi Password: Y9SASASASA

ADDRESS:

Address: [123 MAIN STREET] [CITY, STATE] [XXXXX]

Google Maps Navigation URL: (google maps location link)

————Sample Airbnb welcome message————

PARKING:

The property has several self-parking options, the two nearest parking garages are:

1. Radisson Blu Hotels & Resorts, The Royal Mile, 80 High Street, City of Edinburgh, EH1 1TH (3 minutes walk) – approx. $24/24hrs

2. NCP, Edinburgh St Johns Hill, 2 Viewcraig Gardens, City of Edinburgh, Edinburgh, EH8 9UQ (8 minutes walk) – approx. $16/24hrs

Parking charges are not included in the price of your Airbnb booking.

GROCERIES:

The nearest grocery store is a 5 minutes walk from the flat.

You may use this URL for navigation to the store [GOOGLE LINK]

Address: [INSERT NAME AND ADDRESS OF CLOSEST GROCERY STORE]

PREPARING YOUR PROPERTY

Emergency Exit Instructions: Head out of the main stairwell and exit through the main door.

EMERGENCY NUMBERS:

Police (non-emergency): [INSERT NUMBER]

Police, Fire, Ambulance (emergency): 911

WASHING MACHINE:

If you need to use the washing machine, please refer the user manual at the following link:

https://www.ikea.com/gb/en/manuals/renlig-integrated-washing-machine__AA-1609380-2.pdf

DISHWASHER

Please refer the dishwasher manual at the following link

https://www.ikea.com/au/en/manuals/rengora-integrated-dishwasher__AA-1402781-2.pdf

I would also like to remind you of the House Rules:

- *Please respect the home and look after it as if it was your own.*
- *Take care not to stain or damage the walls or floors.*
- *Anything that is broken should be replaced before leaving or paid to be returned.*
- *Please put all used plates, cups, etc. in the dishwasher.*
- *All windows should be closed when you are not in the apartment.*
- *Please place all used towels in a pile on the bathroom floor before you check out.*

—————Sample Airbnb welcome message—————

LOCAL RECOMMENDATIONS:

If you are looking to hire a car during your trip, I recommend Turo. It's like Airbnb for vehicles, and if you use the following link to register, you will get $20 off on your first hire

[INSERT URL]

If you are planning to take a day tour to the [LOCAL ATTRACTION] tour is considered one of the best, and you can book it from this link at the lowest price: [INSERT URL]

You can purchase [LOCAL] Sightseeing Hop-On Hop-Off bus tour here https://tinyurl.com/EdinburghHopOn

At this link, you can pre-book Edinburgh Castle tickets at no extra cost and skip the queues https://tinyurl.com/EdiCastle

You can see the full list of tours and local activities at this link https://tinyurl.com/BestOfEdinburgh

I hope that you will have an enjoyable stay in [CITY NAME]!

Best regards,

[YOUR NAME]

Trash Policy

- **Trash Pick-Up Day is Wednesday (7 am). Please place trash cans outside of** the property on TUESDAY evening.
- All trash must be put in trash receptacles
- All trash must be placed in a plastic trash bag and placed in the trash bin.
- Do NOT put trash directly into any trash can, it must be in a trash bag.
- If you are residing here on TRASH PICK-UP DAY (Wednesday)
- You are required to put the cans in front of the home and bring them back in on Wednesday evening.
- Do NOT leave the trash cans in front of the home longer than 24 hours.
- All dirty diapers must be put in a place and sealed in a small plastic bag.

CHAPTER FIVE

LISTING YOUR PROPERTY

LISTING YOUR PROPERTY

Do you feel as if you have more clarity on what is needed for your short-term rental business? I hope so. By now, you have learned how to find your property, contract with a motivated landlord or seller, furnish and prepare your property for your guest's arrival, and now it's time to move on to listing your property on the Airbnb website to attract future guests. Let's dig in a bit further.

The first thing that a potential guest will experience when coming across your listing is your photographs. It is essential that you begin by having good images of your property. Having great photographs and attention-catching descriptions will help your home stand out from the rest. You want to make sure they can experience the beauty and warmth from your photos. I always recommend that you have professional images taken; however, it is understood that not everyone will be able to do this for their first properties. This is perfectly okay; just make sure that whatever camera you are using, including your cell phone, you take good quality images. The first set of images can be used as preliminary pictures to get your listing up so you can start making revenue from your listing. However, I do strongly recommend that you take Airbnb up on their offer to use one of their photographers to take your images. You will see an option that says "want professional photography" click this button. You can click that button and make an appointment for a professional photographer to come out to the home and photograph the home for you, and it will boost your listings up, and it only costs around $100 to get this done. It's worth the small investment if you want to make your listings pop that people love. The appeal of your photo is what will capture the attention of the person that is scrolling through and looking for the property that they want. The one that looks the best with nice bright pictures and the nice decor people love to see in the listing is the one they're going to choose.

Property Description

When it comes to the property description, I don't believe that you should reinvent the wheel. To make this process easy for you, peruse the Airbnb website and check out the property descriptions for the highly reviewed properties. Look at how the host describes and advertises their properties. Pay close attention to the descriptive words they are using. What are the amenities they are listing? There is already a working model on Airbnb that you can use, and it's not unethical for you to look at the competition and pattern your listing after theirs. After you have done your research, I want you to go and create your own description. Create a word document and copy and paste the titles, description, and whatever stands out to you about the properties that catch your eye. If you can look at a listing and think to yourself, this is a place I would want to stay at; that is a listing for your reference. When it comes to listing your property on Airbnb, there are some great super hosts that have already figured this thing out, and you can do the same ethically by copying some of the things that they have put in their listing and tweaking it to fit your property.

Listing Your Property

Airbnb allows you to list your properties on their website for free. Now before you say there is no such thing as free, yes, it's free to list, but they do take a commission on your booking, and this is how they make a profit. At the time of this book, the rate is 3% which isn't bad considering they host your listing with access to millions of people. They also provide an insurance policy of up to a million dollars if someone damages your property; I think this is a great deal. It honestly makes me feel very secure putting my nice, beautiful properties with my nice furniture on Airbnb because I know if someone comes in and destroys and burns down everything, not only do I have my business insurance policy, but Airbnb also insures their properties as well.

Airbnb is my go-to website to list my properties. You can use this link- https://www.airbnb.com/r/noeller931 when you create your Airbnb account. Remember, it is absolutely free and easy to follow. I also use a few other sites to help ensure my properties are fully booked most of the year. Below is a quick reference list for you.

Quick reference list of websites

- Airbnb - https://www.airbnb.com
- Vrbo - https://www.vrbo.com
- HomeAway - https://homeaway-com.com
- Booking.com
- TripAdvisor.com
- HomeToGo- hometogo.com
- OneFineStay- https://www.onefinestay.com

Pricing Your Listing

Before you list your property, always remember to do your homework on pricing. Visit Airbnb or any of the other websites and research how much properties are renting for. You can easily cross-reference this by using the zip codes for comparison. During your search, allow Airbnb to tell you what the average person is charging for their properties. Because the average person will not be operating this as a business as you are, you can expect to make a little bit more than the average person is making. Doing your research is a great baseline for you; this is called proof of concept.

In addition to helping set your pricing, Airbnb will give you the option of utilizing their Smart Pricing tool, which will automatically update your room rate according to the fluctuations of the demand in your area. Smart Pricing on Airbnb lets you set your prices to automatically go up or down based on changes in demand for listings like yours. When asked if you want this option, the answer is 'yes,' but I want you to keep control over your pricing. Sometimes smart pricing will price your listing too low, so watch out for this. One of the questions they will ask is, what's the minimum that you would take per night? They are going to suggest a ridiculously low number based on your listing. This number will be equivalent to the lowest number offered on Airbnb so that you can get listings. Do not take their recommended tip of what your lowest price should be. You should know what your lowest price should be based on your sales goals. In most cases, you're going to stay around $140 per night with a studio apartment or one bedroom. Your prices will increase for your accommodations with three, four, five bedrooms, or anything larger.

It's important to remain relevant and competitive, so be sure to compare prices of similar Airbnb listings in your area. I'm going to give you some pricing strategies below for your booking calendar, pricing for nights and weekends, and seasonal and holiday sales to help you make more profits on your Airbnb listing. I generally don't share these secrets with the general public or on YouTube, but as I have mentioned throughout this book, I want to make sure you have the tools to create six and seven figures with your short-term rental business. Having the right pricing strategy and knowing when to offer promotional pricing and seasonal pricing is very essential to your business.

Booking Calendar

When listing your property, do not book your listing for the entire year. You want to set your bookings for 90 days at a time. This will allow you the flexibility to change your pricing based on the season. You want to be able to make seasonal adjustments to your calendar.

Weekends vs. Weeknight Rates

When setting your pricing, you are going to make your weekend rates higher than your weekday rates. Weekends are Friday and Saturday, and weeknights are Sunday through Thursday. I price my weekdays generally $20-$30 per night cheaper than the weekend because people will often book the weekends more than the weekdays. This strategy allows me to maximize my profits. For example, if I have a property with an average rent of $150 on the weekend, that same property will be rented for $170. Once you begin to create your sales goals for your rentals, you can figure out on average what you want to profit on each property.

Another secret is to offer discounts for weekly and monthly stays as an option. You want to encourage people to stay longer to ensure your property is booked for the entire month. When listing your property, one of the questions is, do you want to offer a discount for weekly and monthly savings? The answer to this question is 'yes.' There is no exact formula as to how much of a discount you should give but what you want to do is make sure it is a good discount. For example, if your guest rents the property on a nightly basis, let's say at $100 per night, and they rent for the entire month, that would equal $3,000. If they choose the monthly rental, you could offer a $500 discount. If they have the option of a discounted monthly rate of $2500, that would give them enough of an incentive to book with you. You can also apply a discount to any weekly rates.

Using these incentives will help you keep your listing booked with longer-term stays. Longer stays also means more benefits and savings for you as well. You won't have to clean the property as much, and since they'll be at the property longer, you'll have a larger sum of money released at one time. Based on Airbnb's payout, if a guest stays for an entire month, you get paid on the second day that they're there. It's an awesome strategy.

Seasonal Pricing and Holiday Sales

An additional way to increase your revenue is by pricing your property according to your high and low seasons. You should know the high seasons for the area your property is listed in. If you are in a sunny location like Orlando, Florida, the high seasons are Spring

Break and Summer. The summertime is generally a high season as more families travel and take their vacations. Since I have properties in Florida, that is the time that I maximize my profits by raising rental costs. In the winter months, when people aren't traveling as much, I lower my prices so that I can get more bookings. For some properties, winter is a high season. For example, if you are in Aspen, Colorado, where guests go skiing, you will raise your prices and rent more in the wintertime and lower your prices in the summer. The bottom line is you should know the high and low seasons for your properties so you can adjust your prices based on the season.

Just like a retail store, you should also run promotional and seasonal sales. People love a good sale. When you run a promotion, be sure to raise your prices and then apply your discount. For Holiday sales in your listing description, indicate the special you are running. For example, Spring Sale, Summer Sale, Christmas Sale, Valentine's Day Sale, etc.

These are the strategies I use to maximize my success in this business. I hope you also find these helpful. Remember, as you list your properties, do your research. Write your sales goals and create a game plan to help you reach your ultimate success.

Visit BNBRiches.com to get access to my course that will teach you more secrets on how to make money with short-term rentals along with FREE weekly training calls included. Use code "50OFF" for huge savings!

CHAPTER SIX
MANAGING AND GROWING YOUR BUSINESS

MANAGING AND GROWING YOUR BUSINESS

Future Millionaire, are you ready to put everything you have learned so far into action? Does this seem like a business you can grow and manage? I hope these tips are resonating with you and getting you excited about reaching your financial goals. In this chapter, we are talking about how to manage and grow your business. Now you may be thinking, *I'm just going to get me a couple of properties*. And that may be okay if you don't want to create wealth with short-term rentals. But I have to be honest and let you know that if you want to have the lifestyle that you desire, one with a six or seven-figure income and your unlimited freedom, I do not recommend that you just start with one or two properties. Your goal should be to reach at least $10,000 a month in income so that you set this up as passive income that doesn't require much time and energy. I even suggest setting your annual goals even higher to $250,000 to $300,000 per year, because that is really the sweet spot in America when you have that $20,000 to $30,000 per month in income. But again, you know your needs. These are my goals for you but of course, you have to set your own goals.

An important part of running a successful short-term rental business is organization. Checklists will be your best friend. Your checklists will include all of the things that each property needs. You must be organized so that you can grow your business. Use the checklist and templates that I have included throughout this book as samples to guide you. Make sure you print off copies and use them as you build and manage your business. As a growing business, you will need to keep account of your rental availability. You will also need to know if there are any issues that have occurred in your rental property. You'll need to ensure the property is maintained and cleaned. You'll need to have your inventory monitored before and after each guest check-in. It is up to you to ensure that the needs of your homes are handled in a professional and timely manner.

Trusted Partners

Trusted partners will be essential to you having a successful short-term rental business. The reason I say "trusted" is because they will have access to your keys and your property to look after things for you. When running a 24/7 operation, you'll need to build relationships with people you can trust because you can't be everywhere at once. If you're planning on running this business remotely there are three key people that you're going to need to help you with the maintenance of both the property and day-to-day operations. These partners do not need to live in the same building as the property but they need to be able to access the property at all times.

The first is the cleaning person. Cleaning the property is something that will need to be completed before your guests check-in and after they check out. I don't expect you will have any issues in this area as there are tons of reputable and reliable cleaning companies willing to work. The great thing about Airbnb is you can actually pass that cost directly on to the guests. So, ideally, it's not really an expense to your business.

The next person you will need is a handyman or a maintenance person. You'll need them to make repairs should anything break down or need minor adjusting. If you consider yourself to be handy and you live nearby your property you may be able to handle this while you're growing your business, but eventually, you'll need to hire help. This could be a family member, or it can be a professional handyman that you contract with to do this for you.

Last but not least you will need a customer service person. Now keep in mind you can fill this role but for the sake of this discussion and the future growth of your business, I suggest that you use a team member or someone other than yourself. The customer service person will keep in correspondence with the guest. They are also the person that will be called on to handle any issues. For example, if the guest loses their keys to the property, if they lose the garage door opener, or they are locked out or have any other type of emergency, the customer service will need to be available and willing to help resolve the issue both professionally and quickly. You want to be strategic about who handles this position. This person becomes the representative of your property and sometimes, they will be required to have face-to-face interactions with your guest. Make sure to choose someone who is dependable and does not live miles and miles away. The last thing you want is for a guest to have an issue and no one can access them for hours.

Growing with Guest Reviews

To manage and grow your business, you will also need to manage your business image. The short-term rental model is no different than your traditional business model. Happy customers, a great product, and marketing and promotions are also needed in the short-term rental business as well. To earn a lot of money and pocket big profits you must bring value to your customers. In the short-term rental world, your image is managed by the amount of 5-star reviews you receive. 5- star reviews are solid gold.

Many hosts don't know that the more five-star reviews that you receive, the higher your property will show on the search on Airbnb. It's very easy to obtain a five-star stay if you are deliberate and you make sure that your properties are clean, safe, and comfortable. Your 5-star reviews will tell potential renters just how valuable your space is. This is the secret to how I make so much money. In short- term rentals value for the customer is offering a property that is clean, comfortable, safe, and secure. In the Airbnb model, both the hosts and the guests can leave reviews about their experiences with one another. You'll leave one to review how they were as a guest, and they will leave your review as to how you were as a host.

How to Get More Five Star Reviews

One of my secrets in getting more 5- star reviews is that I tell the guest that they are going to have a five-star stay when they book their accommodations. That's right before they even step foot on the property, I set their expectations about the experience they will have at my property. This is the same language I want you to use as well to ensure you receive more 5-star reviews than other hosts. The welcome letter template in this book has the verbiage you need. When your guests book, you will send them the message that expresses how excited you are to host their 5-star stay. Guests like it when you communicate with them; this lets them know that you care and appreciate them booking your property.

Once you start getting those 5-star reviews, this is how you will grow your business. Airbnb will reward you by showing your listing to more people. So when you are a host that has 5-star reviews and people love staying at your places, Airbnb has an algorithm that will highlight your property. When people are searching for a property in your area, Airbnb will start to show your listings higher up and show it to more people. This is how you'll get more bookings, and your business will expand more rapidly. Additionally, you will be able to increase your prices. Because you've established yourself as a 5-star host that gives great service, and your properties are very nice, clean, and they have what people need, you'll make a ton of money.

Welcome Your Guest

The last secret that I will share with you to set you apart from other hosts is to make a welcome video for your guest. Now, this is just a recommendation, but it's one from my vault that I use and have experienced great success since implementing it. It adds such a personal touch and makes the guest feel welcomed. Don't worry; this video can be short and sweet, and you don't need to be in front of the camera. I shoot welcome videos with my phone with my voice in the background as I film my property. I am setting you up for raving 5-star reviews with this nugget. By the time the guest steps foot on your property, they would have received the welcome message and a video that shows a lovely way of you going above and beyond. These small gestures and detailed communication will boost up your ratings, which will result in you having more bookings. Then you will be able to increase your price, which results in more profits and additional properties. I am setting you up for success.

Visit BNBRiches.com to get access to my course that will teach you more secrets on how to make money with short-term rentals along with FREE weekly training calls included. Use code "50OFF" for huge savings!

CHAPTER SEVEN
READY, SET, GO!

READY, SET, GO!

Are you ready to begin your short-term rental business today? I hope so! Once you get started, you are going to open up another well of wealth and lucrative stream of income. Trust me, you are well on your way to something great, and I can't wait to hear your testimonial! The demand for short-term rentals on Airbnb remains high. Millions of people are booking every day, and they are looking to rent from people like you. The longer you wait to begin, the longer you will delay your millions, so I am urging you to get started today. Use the scripts and tools I shared with you to help you on your road to making millions with BNB riches.

If you have learned anything from this book and you want a full in-depth course, I have created a completely affordable course that has even more details available for you. You can have access to even more scripts that I use with all of my templates, checklists, and everything that you need to start your short-term rental business for a very affordable price. Just go to BnBriches.com to get started today. I want to make sure that you have all the resources, tools, and knowledge that you need to be successful.

If you need any help on this journey or you want to talk to me or someone on my team, you can schedule a time to speak with us. We can assist you with any part of this process. Starting out, you may have additional questions, and that's perfectly fine.

Let me also drop this last bonus for you. If you decide that you don't want to manage your Airbnb property, you have the option of contracting my company, Nu-uRez. We manage a large portfolio of rental properties. This has been such a profitable model and helped so many of my students that we have set up an opportunity where you can invest, and we can get rental properties for you, and NuuRez will split the profits with you. If you have properties and you need help managing them, we can do that for you as well. You have the option of managing your own property or contracting with a property management company. If you want to speak with my team, visit www.NuuRez.com.

To Your Success!

Visit BNBRiches.com to get access to my course that will teach you more secrets on how to make money with short-term rentals along with FREE weekly training calls included. Use code "50OFF" for huge savings

ACKNOWLEDGMENTS

I want to acknowledge my team that helps make sure that our money-making short term-rental properties are always top tier! To my property managers, quality assurance team, and cleaners, thank you for all the hard work you do.

ABOUT THE AUTHOR

Noelle Randall, MPS, MBA, is an Entrepreneur, Real Estate Investor, Author, Speaker, and all-around leader who is here to help!

Noelle is all about growth. She has been a thriving entrepreneur for over 20 years and is a successful businesswoman, best-selling author, and real-estate entrepreneur. Her diverse business experience has been instrumental in her personal success as well as the success of countless people across the country.

She teaches real estate investing to thousands of people from varying backgrounds who are ready to transform their financial status. Noelle is a full-time real estate investor and founder of the Noelle Randall Coaching Program. She provides training, workshops and hosts events to teach how to start from scratch and build a successful real estate investing business.

As CEO of Noelle Randall Coaching, Noelle offers entrepreneurs business opportunities, allowing hundreds to create wealth and financial independence through her mentorship. She has also created the opportunity to become an owner of properties across the country and obtain passive income for investors of her crowdfunded company NuuRez Inc." Additionally, Noelle is the Executive Director of the Marley Simms Foundation, a public, non-profit organization dedicated to promoting children's literacy. Its mission is to advance the diversity of thought in children by providing access and awareness to books from diverse authors and discussing diverse topics.

Noelle is the founder and president of FDR Horizon Enterprises, a private real estate equity firm, and brand manager. The company owns a diverse portfolio of real estate and has created numerous profitable and top-selling brands, including her signature product, Tea More Skinny (TeaMoreSkinny.com). In addition, Noelle is the co-founder of Bella J Hair (BellaJHair.com), the premier virgin hair extension brand and international hair and wig distributor.

In addition to being a tenacious entrepreneur and businesswoman, Noelle considers herself a perpetual student, always learning and growing. Noelle proudly boasts two advanced degrees. She earned her Bachelor's Degree from the University of Connecticut in Urban Planning. She has a Master's Degree in Economic Development from Penn State, and most recently, she earned a Master's in Business Administration (MBA) from Baylor University.

Noelle is also the proud mother of seven children, whom she credits as her inspiration for every endeavor.

CONNECT WITH NOELLE

Noelle Randall, MPS, MBA, is an engaging, transparent, and powerful speaker for audiences wishing to learn real estate and live the lives they have always wanted.

Noelle is always willing to help and teach new methods and techniques to those who might actually need them. She incorporates her teachings into her life. She does not hesitate to educate people about the secrets to becoming a millionaire in real estate. Her goal is to help and make more people become millionaires like herself.

Noelle is devoted to helping more people, and she can be sought through her website www.noellerandall.com or her social media accounts:

facebook.com/noellerandallcoaching

https://twitter.com/noelle_randall

https://www.instagram.com/noellerandallcoaching/

https://youtube.com/c/noellerandall1

Email: contact@noellerandall.com

Made in the USA
Monee, IL
07 October 2022